THE P

D0686565

Jacques Roubaud

THE PLURALITY
OF WORLDS
OF LEWIS

Translated by Rosmarie Waldrop

Dalkey Archive Press

Originally published as *La pluralité des mondes de Lewis* by Éditions Gallimard, 1991. © 1991 by Éditions Gallimard.

English translation © 1995 by Rosmarie Waldrop.
First Edition, 1995

Some of these translations first appeared in *Central Park, lin/go, Long News for the Short Century, Manhattan Review, New American Writing, Notus, Pequod, Shearsman, Talisman,* and in the exhibition catalog of *Documents IX* (1992).

Library of Congress Cataloging-in-Publication Data

Roubaud, Jacques.
[Pluralité des mondes de Lewis. English]
The plurality of worlds of Lewis / Jacques Roubaud ; translated by Rosmarie Waldrop. -- 1st ed.
p.   cm.
1. Grief--Poetry.   I. Title
PQ2678.O77P5813   1995   841'.914--dc20   94-7327
ISBN 1-56478-069-4

Publication of this book was made possible in part by grants from the French Ministry of Culture, the Illinois Arts Council, and the National Endowment for the Arts.

Dalkey Archive Press
Campus Box 4241
Normal, IL 61790-4241

NATIONAL
ENDOWMENT
FOR ♥ THE
ARTS

Printed on permanent/durable acid-free paper and bound in the United States of America.

Contents

Author's Note

The title of the book (as of its first section) is taken from David Lewis's *On the Plurality of Worlds* (Oxford: Blackwell, 1986).

The fourth of the "Circles in Meditation," "Flowers, Flower," was composed by plagiarizing and rearranging chapter 31 of the *Essay des merveilles de nature et des plus nobles artifices* of R. P. Etienne Binet (1632).

In the third, some passages in quotes (not all, but it is easy to tell which) are borrowed (others transposed without acknowledgement) from Giorgio Agamben (*La comunità che viene*, Einaudi, 1990). They are twisted from their original sense (a double twist, since all quotation—and some of his fragments are themselves quotes—is a twist), which admission I hope will make him (at least half) forgive me.

THE PLURALITY OF WORLDS OF LEWIS
1987–1990

(i)

A body and its shadow shared a world

The shadow's shadow spread over the body

This world was the fusion of possible shadows

And the shadow of each part of this world was itself a fusion of this world, and only of this world

Shadow, the fusion of shadows make for a living world

When shadow and shadow of shadow no longer merge into one world that world is dead

(ii)

It will be objected that possibly there is nothing rather than something

And that, if a world is the maximal fusion of all the shadows it contains, there is possibly, through invisible reflection as well as involution, a world that is absolutely empty

But a world is not a bottle from which light escapes like smoke

A world is a necessary truth, not an explanation

There is no empty world, a world is not even empty when reduced to a point that is indescribable,

Disappearing, homogeneous, unoccupied.

(iii)
Transworld

There is no transworld travel

Nor any transworld traveler dragging his world along with him

There is neither revoking of duration, nor consciousness before time, nor any special way of surviving the sudden lack of direction

I wake up at night, I see the backside of the world

but this is not the way to reach you

(iv)
The World of "Pictions"

A cat, its photo propped against the books, among the books

nothing hidden, no small hidden sense making for

insubstantial additions

neither a head
                    bathed in the gold of evening

nor the solid, the white

between doors that seem stuck

on the moment when a breath began

a lid on this eye lifted

he will not see again   around, nor below
        the angle hidden in smoke
                    yet, it was here

(v)
The Way of Examples

by Way of Example:

is a number now less concrete than your body?

trees, lights, islands, Xeroxes,

but a number?

of a pure order, irreducible to empathy

your hand?   your hand, not otherwise,
    ungraspable

(vi)*

Clean world, clean world, not deceptive, but absent

if it is absent, it is nowhere, you are nowhere, and that's that.

in a clean world you were, you could be: not here but there; or not there but here; or here then there; there

in a clean world there were countless ways to be

all other worlds are "rubbishy."

this world: infinitely rubbishy; in absence made mine; but you

may be, in a clean world, indiscernible from it, and I

looking, through an infinity of worlds,

for one

---

*English version by Jacques Roubaud.

(vii)
World of Our Few Years

World of our few years,   curve

red already above the orbit
        gone cold

and hard lines

down into the dark

in my hand under the cloth

in your hand and squeezed

by it (your hand)   down to you

suddenly inhaled, before us

an estuary

of fresh

cool air

(viii)
The More-than-World

beyond what you can say

every point, and word, every term, and more charged, more in-
sistent

body doubled by shadows, redoubled and reshadowed

full globule, space falling in counted

drops, a continual recount

the first come and the first come again and the last

gone and come again

as first, seen from below

all this which, into the bargain, is no more than the world

alike up to a certain moment, they diverged.

you would explain (would have explained) it thus

we were two segments of a world, each the other's "double," *doppelgänger* in a biipsistical relation.

maximal segments of a world, so that there were none larger and still alike: "myself, like you."

up to a certain moment.

up to a certain moment (you'd have explained it thus), in a back and forth of quips: centuries, weeks, cities, galaxies, nights and rooms: we had all that.

the two simultaneous, more-than-alike worlds were intertwined

it's not so much, you would have said, that they diverged, but

that transworld relations were cut off once one world ceased

once one world ceased, and the moment of separation started to recede.

(x)
The World of Haecceitas

it would make sense to hold that <u>this</u>
   could be extended to any logical space
   with all its inner oneness, tone and self-expression

that no blurring could be forced

on what, once it is <u>this</u>, would have been such

in at least one world, and recognized

across all dissimilarities

as against scatter, against dissolution, against the silence of
   what's not pulse, but emptiness

(xi)

Via Negativa:

no place

moments impossible to discern

refusal of fused shadows

pure multiplicity unexampled

unsupported roofs

(xii)

windowpanes and gold in silent alternation

windows, conditional escape routes,

evening, but then which day's evening?

the world won't tell me, won't tell this:

it is a world as it were pushed

out of an empty artery still pulsing weakly,

or a branch veering barely

from its trunk, of little sap, dry, stripped of leaves.

split light, alike,

each alone, quite alone, tin mouth

this evening which, no matter

where I am, won't let me sleep.

(xiii)
Walls, Three O'Clock

for so many reasons this world, ours,
    is impossible

how can it be an instance of what should
    be so that a world could be?

but if there are many worlds, and every
    way that a world could possibly be is a way
    that some world   is

if whenever such-and-such might
    be the case

there is some world then where
    such-and-such is,

this world, ours, the least likely, is possible:

but reading it on this void does not mean I believe it.

(xiv)
Ersatz-World

living in an <u>ersatz</u>-world.

each detail concrete, exact, just as it is; or might have been.

correct world.

trees outlined against a dust of rain

the moments of the <u>ersatz</u>-world the sharper for their difference

colors disappear into their complements

(xv)
The Sphere

how many nights I've locked myself

inside this chalk sphere, but no demon

came to place me instead

in another verifiable life—yours,

a place of holding, sharing,

of warmth, neighbor to words

with night, crumpled and smoothed, for sheets.

no serious demon answered my call and

filled it with a palpable form

called back from territories

colorless, inconceivable, unending.

not even when for one single selfsame night

I threw into the bargain my own death.

(xvi)
In the _Ersatz_-World

or our world, perhaps, presented as <u>ersatz</u>

to our eyes nothing but
    understudies in the role of things

yet an impeccable <u>ersatz</u>-world, its own replacement, correct

banner of rooted certainty: that it is there, that it occupies the
place by itself, all places:

that this wall is a wall, beyond hypotheses;

                    but you,
    you might not have been at all, not this . . ., nor this . . .

worlds that the verbs hurl at us
    on approval

(xvii)
Any, Any Whatever

there is no place, not even in myth, of which we could speak
truly, if with contradictions

not even, it's an old tale, the place of nowhere.

someone, however, speaking of you in your grave

it does exist, the earthly portal of that place,

it does exist, the grainy stone,

but I could not even claim <u>nothing</u> was <u>there</u>

could not find any modality to curtail

(xviii)

Where time imitates a solid line, several copies of a solid line, each of infinite duration, put end to end.

Each copy of the world that follows each other copy in each infinite and solid line of time repeats the preceding world identically.

The same world it is,   composed of indiscernibles.

From one world to the other, from the objects of one world to those of the other, no distance but an infinite of moments of separation.

No distance to cover, an immobility sufficient but infinite.

Thus I'm now in the same world still, I've covered the infinite distance of separation, and nothing will ever be familiar again.

(xix)
The Way of Stories

if worlds were stories, their inhabitants storytellers,

not just the living beings, but all, all things, all

telling their stories, all being told

there would be room for worlds

where contradictories could be true

where I could say "you live, you're dead"

and with a laugh, you would reply

(xx)
The Way of the Impossible

the impossible is not the case in any world.

in any world everything, always, can only be possible.

nothing impossible can be said

otherwise, elsewhere

except by saying.   I hold nothing back

by saying: "you."

and I show nothing either.

(xxi)
What to Do with a World

What to do with a world that we don't speak of

that nobody had, or has, anything to say about, nothing

not one detail, not one particular occurrence with description
attached

a world so extremely general

that the unique, the unrepeatable, is abrogated

from the moment no one understands

the moment no one knows what to do with in his mouth

to get around this word, oust it in one syllable

spit it out with disgust

a world abominably imprecise

that I must live with

that I must always be looking at?

(xxii)
Bright World

bright world, ferrous lights, slopes

sun turning in the water

I open my eyes, notice the weight

of the heat on my eyes and hands,

the air brilliant, but short-lived.

world frozen in a transparent

present, turning on itself

yesterday dark, dense, opaque

tomorrow opaque, dense, dark

bright world, waystation

resting place

without dimensions, your image passing through.

(xxiii)

In these worlds, in every one, beings forever without signature,

whom nothing, nothing can lift up or drain, nor mark, nor put
in place

dust, bodies extended, convertible stroke by stroke
masses of some neutrality

did we have to take the trouble to posit

modest axioms of rationality

that would round out these forms, these figures

(infinites of calculable thickness)

(comets used as diapers)

and clothe their aridity

in true greenery or moral agents

(xxiv)

"alive, absent from all life"?

where is this world?

"living a different life elsewhere"?

but who?

"everywhere," this empty box

"no one," this diamond consumed

like memory of a cat left in the air
          after a wash of noise

I squeeze my fingers around the colorless

flame that burns and burns this image.

Inside the image

where the sheet discovers you

where your finger chars, a bath of ashes

(xxv)
Division of Worlds

this world: split in two, two irreducible, unconnected space-times.

in one of the two halves, all points are joined from arc to arc; in the other, likewise.

but between them nothing, not even an arrow: impassable space.

one cannot cross from one sub-world to another,   one cannot cross alive.   or dead.

Me here, you there.   not together.   over there I'm dead

Over there no more than here, we are no longer in the world together

(you will die there, I here)

In return you are,   are   there,   still.   It is the only consolation. Survival is too big a word.

(xxvi)
The Way of Examples, II

where shall we draw the boundary between number and penumbra?

certain pieces of world are <u>this</u>: ink, protons, stars

but a number?

and of which suitable species, you, now?

where, between the unicorns and winged horses we can enumerate?

in the penetrable limbo of a hedge?

in which entire world, shadowy enough in spite of its eternity?

so I tried, again, by Way of Examples.

(xxvii)
Lyrical

swaying line of leaves

the tops of seven English poplars in the distance

beyond the blue and green space

concede your dissolution.

unlikely that I thought, in June,

when those far tree tops and your bush, peak

of nudity, waved to me under the warm

tongues of windows filling with sun,

how brief those mornings were, and how equivocal.

I knew it, I remember, a beautiful day,

with that beauty of air that says nothing,

puts hours in our hands and vanishes.

how warm the smell of the short grass, crushed

and covered

by your legs.

(xxviii)
That the World Was There

Falling asleep I saw the world was there,
the world and all that follows from it;
"now" smaller than a point
behind immense and serious colors.
buzzing years come back from afar,
angle of street and street,
traces washed off by rain,
yellow stuff gathered in my hand.

In falling asleep I saw all this:
the warm ellipse of the well,
the earth where leaves have no more weight,
the water, level, median, in balance.

I saw, falling asleep, I saw
what I had welcomed now for years
but what my memory did not know:
entire years with truth,
that is, if you insist, with death.

I did and did not want to see, falling asleep,
what I had seen too many times.

(xxix)
Plenitude

all that a world could be, no matter what,

is, somewhere, in some way.

fullness of possibles, consistency.

no matter which talking head, mine

for example, adjacent to my body

and

why not

against my face, the angel's, the black shadow face itself,

but all the seats are taken, all the worlds

unavailable

to you.

(xxx)
Identity

What identity could be yours, that of your death?

you are, some would say, your grave and its inside,
    the gravestone with your name

but that only means saying:

alive, you were this body dressed and undressed,
    this body that contained your thought (or soul)
    this body that also bore this, your, name

identity does not last in the world except by this analogy

you are, others would say, as you are in the memory,
    if they remember, of those who had,
    even just for a moment, known you

thus you would be, but parceled out, changeable, contradictory, dependent, in intermittent light,

and once all those are dead you would no longer be.

and, surely, here again the idea of afterlife borrows its very characteristics from the world that was your life

but for me, it is quite different:

each time I think of you, you cease to be.

THE SICKNESS OF THE SOUL
1986

The Sickness of the Soul, I

We think, it was believed, under an effort of the air

Moon eye on the left, sun's on the right

and pain comes

the changes from what to what

my legs tremble when I come near a match

my hands tremble when I raise a shadow I shouldn't have raised:

fear, shame, sorrow, fervor, anger   all the rest

that in a body suits reunion, among other things, sweats, disorders of the heart,   the rest.

Thus air spreads through the channels of the body, mum about its strength   as about all that it conveys of warmth and lack of understanding.

The Sickness of the Soul, II

What is nameless within you   must thus be named

hidden under the warmth, under the air, the breath

under a layer of moist stone pierced by stars

Ambushed by the light, this small epilepsy

tormenting my moves away from your hips

a moment washed clean of scatter and pain

and this time one more time

to approach this being

hidden all right,   but spurning surface finish

The Sickness of the Soul, III

Light accompanied by wordless sorrow

deathly crags that an isthmus mends

her lungs, the lichen of her heart

red, the light partaking of her fingers partaking of the air

sand shifting on its hinges

fright

the cutting joy

so smooth, so bright,

before the mirror rough with wrinkles

The Sickness of the Soul, IV

The stars defenestrate
My mouth opens to the amoral sun
Horrible intimate birds
Scratch at the leaves
The snow, the lamp, the lemon, the red

I had not counted
On these details: the traces of your body
Such massive instability
Under glass
Diluted from the core   the shoulders   night   orbits

Daylight, brief at first
Caught in the blue bowl
The clay   the silvering   the lamp   the sealskin
All you never anymore are

Air, Water, Places

Memory makes the body unlike

the flesh received into eternity

the fears prepared to finish with it

it opens to an end without finality

the moment that the cold spells out

curbing her mouth to cover it

with earth where the right to space

to pleasure and to time is lost

as is her face, slavering inconceivable grass

Air, Water, Places, II

Turning from yourself inside yourself

divisible into specific pains

diffuse

outside the similar   ousted by the not-different

brief, multiple   to the edge of nothing

once you no longer thought yourself inside another

never again informed by one-way dreams

that channeled the uncomfortable light

its movement opaque against your neck, your ass, your stockings

Air, Water, Places, III

lack of sun and snatched from

flesh unbounded in experience

the dark is made of wooded plains

presses against your palm irradiates it

moist, it bows to the irruption

while the gasps build thick and fast

to earthquake force

undoing it does not deflect the thought of death

when words once more pour through the body

The Sickness of the Soul, V

I raved, but gently, being of polite and peaceful disposition

a green meadow sloping gently toward a brook was constantly suggested to me

fall plunged into winter there, demonstrably

outside the window the park (Chiswick) divided into two dark halves

the picture she'd composed from this window was also split in half by a white stem ending in a thicker tip

this symmetry undid what little comfort might have been offered by the receding double mass of gloomy, dripping English trees

the stem in the picture began to resonate with the incongruous desolation

out of winter's mouth, mist escaped like an enraged

soul, and spring, in turn, approached with empty glasses

Air

The blade of straw on the blanket, tufts of wool a hand invented on the wall, tomb of the first sun. Fall of summer.

Stifled red of clouds, but the sky did not itself add, one by one, these qualities, Proprietor of redness, she inhabits and composes it.

Carried back into the lamplight, successive changes memorized, there were several designs for a world.

On an evening of burst leaf and relative beings

Where every action was an increase of the same

Ground measured by fever, her face turned to the wall

Every drop of air imploded, leaving her a bit emptier yet

Until, once more for the first & last time, the miraculous correlation of coffee and new day.

Ink Simulacrum

    This chemical trace looming with the hugeness of objects that
encroach on a different duration

    what a way to say: this is "you"?

    if even when I close the eyes outside my skull
if memory   projects

    on their imagined retina
an image bathed in moments from before your death

    but in a sense the opaque
quasi-black

    with economic movement
with pale colors cedillas

    a plunge inside a white collar

    if   I said   I stir up
this ink simulacrum
in my head

    what will
I gain?

Preparatory Poem

the spent, red evening escaping out the window

(it had come suddenly, the shadows had not even had time to take inventory of their ties).

the evening we did not know, even while possessing it

chalk   of the windowpane   bombast of facades

dust trembling in the outskirts like a consolation

smoothing our eyes,   the docile air

the forms, pictures, voices, concordance of leaves getting late

light perceived as direct, precarious, through the lungs

and the world once more what it could have been in the first century of photography.

Memory

memory: born late

unbroken body   real and infinite beings

far from the moment marked by pain

from recall not wanting me to forget

from recall not forgetting what I want

memory shot through with nights

time rebuilds around a voice

unnamed surfaces   mate with the nameless

space finally bonds, duplicating itself

CIRCLES IN MEDITATION

Meditation on Himself

Nothing more distressing than this daylight, nothing hazier. So you would paralyze the brightness? You haven't yet broken the spell of sleep, and already you're discomfited by noise and, trickling through the noise, your first terrors ruffling the silence. You see the wall, but stained with cold, spoiled with lines: and you among them. You feel a movement at the window, and you sluggish, without strength, frozen. All of death in perfection, and you raw, still at the very first point of considering the day and yet already wishing for its end so that sleep could finally take better care of you than you can.

Look, and look again, at this slow light on which depends the management of things and your movements. And you heavy, hesitant, divided, hurt, it seems, by the slightest refraction, the slightest trammel. Your head, once the site of forests and illuminations, could be crushed by a fingertip's lightest touch; your bones collapse under the mere weight of the sky. Your mouth already clogged with words tasting of lead before you've said a thing.

So what is it to you, this newborn day? This day of which they say that night, its mother, miscarried from the mere sight of your lamp put out? Such a great thing, the night, perish for so little? And for what? A feeble light so far, but which, the moment it takes form, disheartens your eyes. It gives you headaches, vertigo, blinding flashes, nausea, arrows of pain on the side of the heart.

Listen, you mass of doubt. Retrace your steps, remember the hours without ceiling, consider the disasters of your life there, in the considerable darkness. Turn, little slip of mortality, turn your eyes toward the gloom that chokes you in the seed, in leaf, in mock bloom; and weigh carefully its fruits that never ripen. Night, alas, but real night and nothing more, retrench within this lawn of gloom where you are planted, confine yourself to the surrounding air, stop trying to escape its desert and get used to yourself.

Where were you before the day? In very nothingness, with nothing more than yourself. The branch of your anxiety was grafted there: and you on it, but on its terms; it always different, and you different; it full of the world's opprobrium, you full of it. That's how you were. Nothing, but nothing scratched you with thorns, nothing rusted you through, nothing spewed you from clouds of smoke. You saw all that. You could not speak, move, do over. This went on. Hence these tears.

But the coming day will be worse, you think? The light offends you, lies in ambush, you say, attacks you, punishes? You can think of nothing else. Every movement you begin, the light anticipates to the point of scattering you, biting. Here it comes now around the edge of the door, swells the window, lays siege. What would you not give to stop it. Then it would all stop, you think. But how?

Why do you, under these conditions, measure how near the dusk? Why do you work so hard to understand the forms darkness has comprehended in so little space? What is it about all this dark that absorbs your anxieties? You see the heavy mass of darkness, you judge it boundless within you, you cannot see the end, and your judgment is bound up with this boundlessness.

The dark does not vanish in obedience to your eyes? Its points have no thickness, its air no volume? It is no more distant than the wall opposite, where you recognize nothing? Even if the cube that envelops you were as vast as the sphere of stars once believed fixed, even then your eyes would deceive you as to its volume, would judge it minuscule or, if you prefer, inexhaustible. And from this state of uncertainty, you would retreat to a still greater ignorance, for the simple reason that you would not know it?

On your left, the window that daylight will soon find no matter what you do. Hesitant now the light, now the dim objects, now both. Everything begins to shift, with imperceptible imbalance and without a trace of grandeur. Before the sun, nocturnal images disperse. They were there first, but once there is sun they are no more. Where are, already, the trees you took care to see among them? The flowers? Like soil that had its cover whipped off by winter, night strips bare the moment it abandons you and leaves you blind, terrified, to daybreak.

You close your eyes. The eyes open inside your body hold no horizon, but neither do the eyes locked under your lids. You do not see, you are seen. All of the light gathers in order to observe you. Get out of your eyes, because it is already there. Get out of the beginnings if you can: the beginning of sight is the first limitation of sight, its form, another. Look for some essence of sight that has neither beginning nor form, but gives both beginning and form to what you are looking for. Be done within this infinite that subsists on itself. Look and judge this vision compared to which everything visible is only a point of light at the price of the sky, only a nothing at the price of an all. Look there.

Your hands heavy on your eyes. Would you have believed this paltry vision? As soon as your hands withdraw, as your fingers stop pressing, the mirage is gone. Rub with your palms where the tears are pricking. The air already brighter. On your right, the door. On the left, the windows: one window, and another. You see them out of the corner of your eye: extreme smallness of your world.

For now you've come full circle back to the moment of entering this meditation, you are again at daybreak, in its paralyzing light. But what have you learned? Having nothing, what could you expect from reflection? That a few minutes pass, that the abyss of panic be followed by resigned anticipation of certain habitual gestures: turn out the lamp, pick up your clothes, swirl and shake the liquid in your cup, so much effort for so little gain?

The anxiety remains. The light hazy. Where am I if not here? And if here, how bear it yet again, this day, another day? The thickening noise and the light that defines, outlines, fills the room, leave me hollow. I do not recognize myself in them. I squeeze with impotent fists the shell of a virtual almond, a bubble of infinitely thin glass, trying to crush them. But they resist.

And I look, and look again, at this slow light on which depends the management of things and my movements. I strain, not toward thought but surrender, not toward time but duration, to fill it, sew it up. The light knocks, and I open. It gives me nothing, but I have asked nothing, promised nothing. I do not want to see it, but what can I do?

Night is now closed to you; you have forgotten even its frightful mire which, however, you would not give up. Why? Because you were embedded in it without your other you, a you alien and entirely absent? Because you were taken in, as if in spite of yourself, for a patience without pity, a pain without responsibility? Because you did not have to answer your own: what have I done?

It is summer, but drawing near its end; the light comes later now, I feel it. It is morning, skipping a page, the edges a little more eaten by ink, blurred. Night is getting longer. Even if you do not stay in bed alongside it, it is there. It makes you move, your bones sluggish, your thinking short of the event.

You wait for winter, for more than winter: a northern life, in limbo, without confrontations. So you do not really prefer sleep or non-light, nor do you really fear the light or waking up, but rather the transition. The smallest transition hurts you, the smallest transfer, because then there are images that track you and reverberate. And for this paltry discovery you have saddled yourself with consciousness rather than confusion?

What would it take? That nights draw closer together, that sleep lengthen, suns darken, days attenuate (which they do, of course, which they do), that a time come, to ease you, when you need not drain even the shortest day between each night and the next, because they would no longer be separate?

Even into the Night

Objects began to strip and shed the garment of their form on the last steps still visible outside the dark, wrapping their blunt mass in fabrics of golden transparency. And, heedless of my anxiety, let me see them naked beneath their masks, ever so empty and silent except for their most intimate opacity that they defended to the last.

Their aspect seemed truly that of first, & philosophic, matter, scraped clean of any qualities: which so troubled my mind that I felt myself atremble and on the verge of crying out, so great my surprise and lack of understanding: for I was not calm enough to resist the anxious questions that assailed me from all sides.

Nevertheless I deemed myself almost happy to enjoy this rarest of visions, which at the same time stirred such forebodings of disaster as I could barely endure. But so as not to succumb to something like despair, I kept turning my eyes away from such contemplation, as if it were forbidden.

And the objects, which seemed in some way careful of my ter-
ror (judged unfounded by, but nevertheless giving a certain satis-
faction to, some possible intention behind them), continued to
lose one after another of their individual properties, the scent of
their *haecceitas,* even while still remaining here and there, and dis-
tinct in at least one of them.

Thus furnishing proof of patience and modest shame, I hoped
to escape as an integral subject from the immediate consequences
of these happenings, to be and to remain just an attentive on-
looker on the steps, in the light, where I had paused to watch the
evening. But in spite of my repugnance, I was forced to penetrate
into the dark along with the innocent belongings of the world,
which, as I said, every minute surrendered a larger portion of
their singularities.

And I stood aside, ill at ease, my eyes shifty and unsteady, not
daring to look in their direction for fear of what I might find.

The light, however, real if weakened, continued to probe into the cracks of a wall which, as my eyes adjusted not so much to the color black (the halflight, being both grey and pale, was neither bright nor dark), as to the lack of distinctness, seemed to surround a fountain splashing with naked, trembling nymphs. Perhaps an illusion born of my imagination, my mind still not very capable of bearing the now almost complete dissolution of things.

Indeed, I soon realized that what I had taken for a gathering of nymphs was only a fitful movement of shadows. I had thought I saw a fountain, a liquid jet of tumbling mist and lust, but in fact had before me only an accelerated shrouding of objects now almost reduced to extension and duration. If I were a painter I would have been less anxious.

I made an effort to be calm and, since attributing souls to these disappearances was decidedly not permitted, forced myself to comprise the phenomena under the general category "grey" and to assign them, in purely sentimental, arbitrary gradations, almost satisfactory quantities of "more" or, if necessary, "less."

Who or what could so have denatured the world? I was now certain that where I had left it to climb the porch steps, peaceful in the evening light, there remained only bare disused ribs, porous shells of buildings, enclaves without greenery, and that returning there, even in the unlikely case that I were able to, I should find only useless desolation.

I regretted, O how I regretted the thoughtless impulse that had made me turn my eyes from the hill outlined in red by the insistent sphere of sun in order to follow, higher up, in back, the movement (which had seemed strange) of the fig tree at the dark end of the steps, which suddenly almost resembled the window, the cloud, the shovel left leaning against the *restanque*. Very little time had passed, but I remembered, so it was no longer the same moment.

This was how it began, not the disappearance of things, but their dispossession. (Nothing had disappeared, I was sure; I was, as before, part of this whole, a whole, alas, almost entirely lost because without properties.) Moreover, my memory of this yet so recent moment had something incomplete and changing about it, as if this sickness of objects had begun much earlier, with some kind of incubation period that the splendor and calm of the red evening had kept me from noticing.

Now I could no longer feel the wall, and the light had over-taken me, an almost atonic light that did not draw any color from the faintly vibrating space it reached in the distance.

After this cottony fusion the light itself would cease, I was sure. And I had not enough time left to keep a protective distance, the skepticism of the point that forbids both to think of it in pieces and to conceive of two unlike identities coinciding on it "in time and place."

I could still see, which did not fail to astonish me, given the more and more radical absence of anything to look at. I saw, but what exactly? Shreds, remanences, retinal afterimages of the red vacancy of sun at the far end of the vineyard, where it plunges down into the western valley between the Pyrenees and the Pic de Norre. With these fleeting crumbs, my mind, disappointed by my eyes, tried to dress up the neutral apathy of this "place" that things had molted into. But it did not manage to convince me.

Later, other "objects" already without grain, without surface, skirted me and went on to join an impalpable simplicity, an extension bereft of any definite description. It was still "now," the "now" that had begun with my leaving the steps still in the light to plunge into this anxiety, this empty space, this confusion.

Still later, there was an irreducible, new, <u>other</u> moment. Because it would be unrepeatable and the last oneness, I entered into it. I advanced with closed eyes, but still saw before me the same grey, grey-in-itself, the "stuff of the world": a complete void without hieroglyphs or particles, entire, without the smallest change.

Whose pain closed in behind me and accompanied me even into the night.

The Idea of Form

Whether it be truly infinite, or simply beyond my reach, I cannot behold it but asquint, upon a vestige, a delayed effect, a garment, a reversal, a mirror, a shadow or a riddle. *Descort* of any blueprint, I can nevertheless not leave it to chance, nor to any principle that could only distinguish, order or constrain.

Orpheus called it the Eye of the World because it rests on the single inner and outer edge of natural things; Empedocles, Principle of Differentiation; Bruno, Internal Artist. There are many other definitions. For me, it is Infernal Inference (I do not circumscribe it thus, I name it). As soon as you touch paper, as soon as you clear your throat, it cuts in, comprehends, compresses. But without it, the paper would not be touched, or the least sound uttered, let alone heard. Defense everywhere open to loss.

For form cannot declare itself without also declaring the formless, which, however, is not separate from it nor relegated to another place: on the contrary, form cannot but give rise to the formless, cannot but expose its secret inner impropriety.

I have known flawless, brilliant moments when something evident, sharp and simple was to appear to me, was to take on a face; here, the very eveningness of evening, the nightness of night, outside the latent light as much as the diminished dark. Yet I could do nothing.

Commonplace, the sun, commonplace, the earth with all its irregularities, its grass and shingles, its confusions. Red. Absorbed, it seemed, once and for all. But the moment dispersed like the warmth of stone under my fingers.

And my eyes, which kept going back and forth between the assembled tribe of cypresses and the singular line of each tree's presence, without being able to maintain any real demarcation between them, remained stupid.

For form, I agree, is stupid. Substituting trees for the sky cannot absolve it of lack, let alone correct the void, a hospitality that cannot be refused. Neither can saddling ourselves with difficult multiplicity.

To show, at the same time, both an intellectual awareness and a stupefied, dumb absorption of worlds does not promise moral avenues to sight, umbrage to descendants, or etymological support to sentiment.

For all that it is true that form is the only manner, and alone produces samples of things, not essences; whereby it avoids the simpering of sense, the catastrophes of message, as well as the juggling of substitutions. *"Manner is the number and state of things where each remains as it is."*

Form is but the movement whose form it is. Which it does not keep, but shares with all, to become poetry. <u>Thus</u> it is, because "<u>*thus* is what it does best.</u>" It has not happened to be <u>thus</u> (it has no anterior form); it will not happen to be thus (it has no future form); it is "<u>thus, now.</u>" "Now" is poetry.

In the infinitely tenuous present, form moves to set up the "now" of poetry. Here is its infernal inference: to come as near as possible to the demon of silence who "*implores our help.*" (Hence, in the guise of indifference, the modern terror of, and recoil from, poetry.)

It does not say anything. It "would prefer not to." Or again: it does not say except by saying.

All formal poetry is an "unmeasured prelude." Form is carved in <u>filigree</u>, like an absent meter, as if "diaphanous": a light refracted out of darkness. It is lodged in the place of <u>memory</u>: I have said <u>here</u>.

The form of poetry comes out of the irreparable world. It does not build on what "*cannot-not-be,*" nor on what "*can-not-be,*" but on what, <u>at the same time</u>, "*can-(not-(not-be))*" <u>and</u> "*can-(be-and-counter-be).*"

(Chinese, I have been told, makes these distinctions quite naturally as it does not confuse negation and contrary. But there also exists a logic for it that is, on the one hand, very old (Nicolas de Cusa's "not-other than") and, on the other hand, extremely contemporary (Lawvere-Heyting's theory).)

Commonplace, the sun, commonplace, the earth with all its contiguities, its trees and walls, its coverings. Red, black. Fused, it seemed, once and for all. The moment had entrenched itself like the heat of day on my lids.

And my eyes, which kept going back and forth between the assembled tribe of cypresses and the singular line of each tree's presence, without being able to maintain any real demarcation between them, remained stupid.

Flowers, Flower

The seed buried in the belly of the earth, rotted topsy-turvy in the compost heap, winter-whipped, at the first sweet sign of spring rallies its little parts, sends forth little roots to lay siege to the soft clods and suck their marrow, pierces the earth and sprouts a little white shoot, a green nib, feeds visibly, fattens in time-lapse, grows tall,

stiffens a green stem, buds with the Sun's help, secretly digests its colors. The bud swells, pops gently, displaying in the crack its trials of apprenticeship and a ray of time-ripened beauty.

Nature, careful of its fragrant treasures, protects them in curious ways. Some it arms with sharp points, others with bristly burrs; covers these with coarse bracts, sets others under the shelter of huge leaves, winds up secret springs so that, unbuttoned by Aurora's influence, they can rebutton themselves in the evening, before the horrors of night.

Some issue from a green globe, others from a tube, a button, a box, a pannier-shaped basket, a cup, a mottled cushion, a corset, a spike, a bell, a knot, an olive, an eye, a jujube in bloom, a cotton-lined clove, and throw themselves at the light.

The stem is thin or slender or fat, stiff, drooping, smooth, bitter, crenelled, speckled, knotty, or fuzzy, sloughed, sheathed, simple, branching, glossy, gnarled, twisted, leafy, twined, naked, sprouting shoots.

The flower is meager or fleshy or soft, downy, coarse, folded, flat, raised, bulbous, inverted, shingled, cockled, pointed, notched, oval, round, dense, rank, heart- or almond-shape, fretted, bordered, lacy, plain, prickly, with compound beards, with harrows of pointlets, pushing up shoots and hammers toward the tip, turned toward Heaven, bending down to the earth, veined, all one color, flecked with motley, lashed with red veins, bloody, rounded, puckered, slashed, crimped, wrinkled, braided.

Its fragrances countless: sweet, strong, heavy, brusque, bedbug, gloomy, sleepy, quick, delicate, dry, harmful, chancy, mongrel, raspberry, damp, penetrating, fleeting, cloying, acrid, deathly, agreeable, tempered, insipid, saccharine, balmy, aromatic (the scent of the *muscari,* the grape-hyacinth, in the moats of the Cité, down by the ramparts).

tanned, faded, subtle, voiced, unvoiced, circumspect, sharp, flat, soul of scent, hieroglyph, cuneiform, essence, pure vapor, blunt, whipped, fanned, bowed, rain-drowned, wide-awake, sophisticated.

Its color? matte, washed-out, scarlet, purple, persian, violet, high, low, shimmering, soaked, snowy, milky, golden, sapphire, hyacinth, saffron, gold-wash, celestial, sea-green, iris, leaden, blackish, pale green, horn green, thumb green, gold green, grass green, dark green,

Component parts are seed, root, bulb, the fleshy and pulpy node, the first shoot sticking its nose out of the ground, stem, joints, binding, sockets, eye, bud, gum, collar, tear;

appurtenances: leaves, defensive thorns, aglets, filaments, tendrils, bark, marrow, sap, the heart that grows saffron, spurs, spikes, serrations, lace, braids, its weapons: spirit, manna, sap, flair, occult qualities, color, beauty, pleasing arrangement of leaves.

its future: plants, shoots, stamen, pistils, suckers and seersuckers, anthers, foliage, beards, crests, pearls as in imperial crowns.

And its color darkens, lightens, dim color, pale, yellowed, fading, gone, wilted, withered, earthen, rotting, faint, feeble, short-lived, inconstant.

Fall and decline of flowers, the roses, the yellow tulips go to pieces, drop petal after petal, shed their beauty, ruin of gardens, flowers bruised by handling, ripped, torn.

But the seed is found in the pod, the flower's collar, the tip of the filament, the belly, the floss, the fluff, the case, the point of bracts, the spur.

And the seed buried in the belly of the earth, rotted topsy-turvy in the compost heap, winter-whipped, at the first sweet sign of spring rallies its little parts, sends forth little roots to lay siege to the soft clods and suck their marrow, pierces the earth and sprouts a little white shoot, a green nib, feeds visibly, fattens in time-lapse, grows tall,

The Garden of Cyrus

That the elegant ordination of vegetables, which has found co-incidence or imitation in the innumerable diversities of art, yet is also not absent from the mineral world, this is an axiom that, though strangely overlooked by the many, nevertheless belongs within the province of truth.

Could we satisfy ourselves in the position of the lights in our night sky or discover the repetition of the fixed stars to be so invariably soothing if we did not grasp here some imprint of Pythagorical music or the quasi Orphic resonance of a secret crystallography?

But not to look so high or imprison our reasoning in the quincunx of galaxies, observable rudiments of such harmony, transferred by derivation or similarity, are also abundant in subterranean concretions, in gypsum, talc and honeycomb-stone as much as in the crossword imprints of ferns and fossils.

Always, year after year, the same symmetry is deducible from the pendulous excrescences of trees like the walnut, aspen, or poplar which, hanging all the winter and maintaining their network close, by the sudden expansion thereof prove to be the early foretellers of spring; it is discoverable also in the long spikes of pepper, the rustling palms of willows and the flowers of the sycamore or even asphodel, before any fragrance or duplication.

Thus has nature ranged the flowers of sainfoin and honeysuckle, which belongs to Marie de France (or Tristan, if preferred); and somewhat after this manner the beard of the domestic leek, which ancestral superstition enjoined us to set on the tops of houses, as a supposedly invincible defense against lightning, thunder and disaster.

Consider, then, the geometry of the sunflower's flat, lozenge-figured seedboxes, of the pineapple's rhomboidal protuberances, of the pine seed's dictated stiffness dusted with purple resin, the parasol pine's pollen, of the elliptical trajectories in which they spread and scatter over the ground.

For even in ordinary round stalk plants can we read this quintuple disposition, the first leaf answering the fifth in lateral enumeration, just as our loves in season shed their petals in circular patterns. Grass, heather and the fresh shoots of oak trees conform very exactly hereto.

Without omitting how leaves and sprouts which compass not altogether the stalk often cross in alternating long and short diagonals, like the legs of quadrupeds when they amble. This can be seen inexplicably multiplied in the exuberance of poppies, in their chiasmic five-leaved flowers as soon as they are in repose, wrapped for such sleep about the staminous beards, obliquely opening and closing upon each other.

And the buds finally which, awaiting the return of the Sun, do after the winter solstice multiply their interlacings and little figures: lilac stylites, rye, black henbane, lupin.

We conclude from these seminal considerations that the very exiguity and topological unpredictability of seeds in regard to their unfolding is one of the magnalities of Nature (if we understand by this proper name the exercise of genetic memory, which in spite of multiplicatory fantasies is on the whole very constrained). The vast variety of flies or straw does not stem from mutually irreducible monads, but from infinitesimal modifications in rhythmic and sequential bracketing.

The rose at first is thought to have been of five leaves, as it yet grows wild in the fields. But even the most luxuriant, most combed varieties maintain this number in the teeth of any explanation. And everywhere are inscribed within the parenthetical pentagon, as are the vine, the red maple and the fig leaf.

Here some have imagined proof of the mystic nature of this first spherical number and measure of spherical motion, claiming that every globular figure placed upon an even plane, in direct volutation, returns to the first point of contact in the course of its fifth contraction and convolution.

And say that the same number does not only divide the equator of the Starfish, but in that identical order and following identical arrows disposes the elegant semicircles, cavities, spikes and orange tongues of the sea urchin.

Adding further that the circular foundations of the majestic branches of the oak manifest upon incision the pentad signature of a Star; which practice of Nature, become a mystery for art, had once furnished two problems for Euclid.

But the briar, we will say, which sends forth shoots and prickles from its angles, does it not also take care to maintain the pentagonal signature in the unobserved loop of a handsome porch within it? (And let us not forget the five typographic characters in the winter stalk of the walnut, nor the five small buttons dividing the circle of the ivy-berry, with many other observables, which cannot escape the eyes of signal discerners.)

But without spinning this theme further unto numerological extremes not scorned by those whose pentambulatory thoughts we have mentioned, the following proposition will no doubt be more easily accepted, namely that segments of right lines and arcs of circles make out the bulk of plants, whence the profusion of double helices, conical sections, volutes, pyramids and Archimedean spirals (*eadem mutata resurgo!*).

And that (scholium or, rather, corollary—for sure—to the preceding proposition) under these conditions the Flowered Field, to wit the learned herbal of characters that fill the pages of our printed books, far from being simple adjustment of segments and arcs (of which the former directly inspires the I or *iota,* the latter, the O or *omicron*) in proportions derived from the ideal ones of Man's limbs (proof, if needed, of the non-disharmony of microcosm and macrocosm), has its source and metaphor in the art of gardening.

But is this not finally to say that the vegetal alphabet of the stars, its seeds of light flung in a wide flourish as far as the eye of the mind can see, is no other than the one that wafted toward me from the fragrant periphery of grass in the meadow where I lay one warm evening, obliviously, reading, with this meditation going through my head?

Colors Worn

Say this body is light, that body dark. Say it. From one party to the other, the color has suffered tiny modifications. Compare them. To two unequal distances? Two incommensurable numbers? From one to the other, the color has suffered a loss of brightness. But in the one case, there was an internal insistence sustained by time; in the other, surrender, which did not make for continuance.

White paper, flat sheet of white paper whose surface comes from the sky, a sky brighter, whiter, bluer than the white paper, and blue for being white. The sky is less light, the white of the sky less light. Say it. Yet the blue in the white of the paper is also the heavier of the two, the darker; at the extreme opposite of white, falls the weight of the sky, of the blue. Is it the sky that is flat, and the paper, vaulted?

Akahito saw <u>pure white</u> on the top of Fuji, pure white made of snow and a paper cone, white carved on white, a hollow, an eruption? Was it still white? Still pure? Or simply a better white, a little purer than all other white, extremely refined along the neat lines of this vision? Could you tell? Could you say: it was pure white, a bowl of pure snow turned over, and falling?

You say paper looks grey against snow, you say snow looks dark against naked desire (Bernart de Ventadorn: *que la neus quan ilh es nuda par vas lei brun' et escura*). You place a lump of snow under the lamp, here; then away from the lamp, there. Tell us what you see. You see white, but which? The snow burns the paper, the lamp chars the snow; the lump of snow, granted, but the sheet?

In spring, green was the first color. Could you say that? Perhaps. But that, in summertime, green was the indissoluble, intimate union of sky and sunflower, could you, still? And this: that the pines were green, ever green, and that in spring the pines were still green, but a little more so? Had they lost some of their green in the fall? Which? Year after year? Neither the blue-green of yews, nor the yellow-green of pine needles at their root, which is this green that would not veer toward blue, toward yellow?

Say that between red and green all the yellow fades out, say it, Plunge some green, thrust a handful of pine needles into the dark. Burn an oval ball of coal over a mica pane. Pour a jar of pale honey on a pale plate. Think it. Think these transitions. Can you really think this red-to-green, this green-to-yellow? Not this way. How? As lifting off the pine, the anthracite, the honey?

Somebody has superimposed some yellow on top of white, some red, and even some white. Somebody asks us: describe the yellow-white, the red-white, the white-on-white. How are we to take it? I say yellow from this angle, red from that, but the white? What is a white angel on white? I do not understand. I remove the yellow, I remove the red. There is a moment when only white is left. But that changes nothing.

The red was fading steadily, leaving a residual impression of green. You closed your eyes. You opened them. Now it was not green coming off the red, but blue. Once more, it again was blue. And yet once more. But perhaps you had never found any green there? Perhaps the green had only been an illusory imprint as despicably false as a memory?

Suppose then the distinction between green and red annulled. We say green and mean fire, sun, a star's carmine mouth; we say red and mean pines, glaucous water, willows. Sometimes. Sometimes the other way round. All colorblind. No objective correlative, in short, for the separation of "red!" from "green!" Think of this situation: watch how yellow penetrates fields and leaves, how blue gains the cedars, watch the violet petals of the sun. But white?

In the language of my tribe, there are only two words (adjectives, if you like) that can be used for colors: the word x and the word y. The x objects are not y, the y objects are not x, at least if we simplify greatly. And if I say: "this is x" (I am answering your question, you are the one with the tape recorder), is it bright for you? And if it is bright and, according to me, "is y," is it a darker object?

Our sky (my tribe's) is opaque, our snow transparent. Paper is also transparent, paper especially. But sky and paper have the same color (or so we say), and paper the other (there are only two). You play the tape back several times; you scratch your head. You thought that snow and paper were the same color, the color we call x (this is not false), that all white objects were x, and that white was an opaque color. But in fact, we do not have a simple, unnoticeable, undifferentiated sliding from the opaque to the transparent. There is opaque, there is transparent, but there are also four other definite, distinct states that cannot be reduced to these.

The water under the willow, transparent green. The snow on the road, transparent white? This is not possible, you said. But paper? The paper you held against the lamp, through which the lamp light came to you, the paper on which you had written the transparent and green water under the willow, the opaque snow on the road, the snow which, placed on the paper, was melting slowly, was slowly transformed into green water, into background?

90

Colors worn like shadows. Opaque white ground, which under transparent colors takes on their traits. Something white under the color white: does it look white? A white bowl full of snow: pure white, that is to say, blue. But it was the snow that looked blue in the cracks of the roof, not the bowl. The light bounced off it. Snow, puff of pure, transparent water, in the bowl of my hand, through the oval skylight. Seen.

Grey windowpane, difficult for light to pass through. Pain of the light in the grey pane? Grey? Where did the pane get the grey you grant it? Dust, pollution, a tired world, dusk? Choose. Sort the trees, the trees grey with evening, the grey stone walls (*restanques*), the dispossessed, exhausted, motionless things. Then fill the windowpane with white, but without pushing away the world, the outside. You cannot do it.

Water still green, transparent water, pane of transparent green under the willow, limpid, blocking your walk. Green willow in the water, green willow. Clouds on the bottom of the water, the color of water? Green clouds? Look. Cut out the water, watch the clouds, the leisurely clouds, high in the sky, white. Abstract the green of the water, the transparent green. Wind comes down, the water wrinkles, foams, foams white. Pane of transparent white?

Dark white. Say it: dark white. What do you see? Dark red. But white? Embers. But snow? Sheets at night. But winding sheets? Some thing, then, black? Does a thickened silence make noise? Between water and wash? Between the snow surface and the air? Between paper and sky? Volume of air, wooly particles? Filaments of dark? Grey? What do you see? What emerges from the dazzle?

Think of the tribe with only two colors: one color x, the other color y. All white is x. Red, blue, green, yellow are no matter what. And dark white, then? A dark x? A light y? Or colorless like light, like numbers, homeless? Or now luminous, now dark? A "portmanteau" color where they encroach, where x and y overlap? Dark white? And on the other side of this borderline, pure white?

Say white. Say color. Say colorless color. Say black. Say: black sun. You see it: an angel, face of light, against an infinitely narrow wall. This sun bright, that one dark, not black, dark white. Compare them. Compare the colors worn, the deprivation, the setback. Say: white. Say: white sun, white carved on white, carved on the eye. Impossible.

The End of Clouds

pines. I was sitting under the pines across from Sallèles: it was a beautiful evening, the air quiet and calm, the sunset red, without clouds. Everything seemed frozen, bright, immobile. When I looked up, after a long time of staring at the crisscross of pine needles I was sitting on, I had the overpowering illusion of a form that I had seen in the sky before.

days. My days were poorly occupied. Gave little satisfaction to the intelligence. Not only forgetfulness, reflection, too, would have required a different apportionment. The clouds contained the present. They ruled the sky. Their drift charmed me. And in a pinch, at certain moments, they could even make a difference in how the world looked to me.

clouds. My window had been open all night, as usual. Toward four o'clock I was awakened by the pre-dawn and the smell of wet earth, cool and dark. I expected my usual view. But the space between the sky and the hill was almost completely flooded with clouds, the highest and fastest forming their own separate hills amid these plains of forms ploughed by the wind.

forms. If we try to leave off thinking, try to approach the one, infallible absence that absorbs all things, should this not entitle us to participate in the continuity shared by all beings? Unnoticeably, while I was staring, various forms appeared in the confused bustle, swift, incalculable combinations undone too soon for my limited understanding, my heart crushed by evening.

cloud. The thin air without shadows, the solitude of the dry rocks all over the hillside held me. The slope was slanting clay, ocher, almost red, with green veins (paradise of ruined colors). I lay down, my head on tufts of thyme and lavender, my heels against the top of a crumbling stone wall. The sky full, parallel, almost vertical, dotted with one single, round, white cloud.

clouds. As delimited shapes they had to be different from one another. How else could one tell them apart. And yet, to my eyes they could not but form a whole, at least from the moment I tried to take my distance from their medley in order to come to some understanding. From time to time I allowed my eyes to roam, soon defeated by the curve of the earth.

water. A kind of dike formed by trees knocked down by the wind and rotten with age. Alders, aspens and poplars have taken root here. Green wall, impenetrable vegetal wall. However, the <u>Cèze</u> filters through the rubble and comes out with a meringue of foam to form a natural basin of great purity. In it, the light beds down an almost black sky with small cloud complications.

moon. It was noon, a summer day, and the mere choice of these words shows what an as it were ardent atmosphere so much light had extracted from the rocks, the almost exhausted sun, the white, dusty, silent walls. The moon melted into this sky like a light cloud.

equivalents. How could a form, a disposition of air that even with repeated encounters had remained almost entirely alien to me, have such impact on my thinking? Was it that, for a moment, it felt right to let go? or that their randomness allowed me a time of idle waiting?

hours. Heavy, cold, the hours wasted in their pursuit lost all sense of time. They dragged without noise; they were spent without producing anything. The light, once more up in the morning impossible to avoid.

clouds. Even back then I did not like evening, even before it came to resemble dawn. Clouds had the run of the sky. They were of the low-hanging kind, small and monotonous, in quite unnecessary profusion. There was no sound of torrents in incompressible caverns: in other words, no storm brewing. There were only shifting planes.

clouds. Universal harmony, we think, belongs to vastness. We look for it in the clouds because, we believe, it must be there. But where? They have no apparent limits (who would argue from their actual, inevitable dissolve in the mountains or their tumble into the sea) and slip through our fists all the way to the infinite, in the anxiety of our precarious days. Even when their shadow has by chance come to rest on the wall.

cypresses. It was midnight, the moon had set. There was uncertainty on earth. The earth more than dark. Sounds separated by long silence. The cypresses, smoke of an intractable lamp, of dim dust, just barely moved by a breath. Wild garlic. Incommensurate stars. And between.

clouds, solitude. Solitude suited them. Not that they were faltering, but there are different ways of sliding across the sky. I would never have thought that such soft, cottony concentration could be reconciled with such an exigent geometry. But how, without any support, consent to dissolution?

valley of the dam. I very rarely leave the valley between the sun-drenched hills of Sallèles, the valley of the dam, which used to be so leafy, so green before the fire slashed the pines. Half a century ago, I was not afraid to cut through the tangle of reeds and brambles that hides the water. Now, I don't stray from the path. The clouds have not changed. Throwing back my head, I see them as before, scuttling along the surface of the waters of the sky.

poisons. Tea is a great help if you want to be bored in a calm way. Below the rather slow poison of the clouds, a lukewarm cup best suits their unvarying weak emotion. Clouds after rain, like snails in the grass, habits of peace and indifference, liquid weakness that calms the heart:

clouds. Again I was sitting under the pines across from Sallèles, a repeated target for my local sadness. I suffered not only from oblivion, but also from the deep space between sky and hill, almost completely flooded with clouds. Trying to leave off thinking, to approach their absence, I lay down, my head on tufts of thyme. To my eyes, they could not but form a whole where the light bedded down an almost black sky.

window. Soon I had but the choice of these mere words to show this disposition of air which all my life had remained almost entirely alien to me, even though I had wasted so many hours of my time in their pursuit. The clouds had the run of the sky here, in universal harmony with vastness. My window had been open all night. Earth more than dark.

Cartwright Gardens: A Meditation

Once or twice or three, four times a year, I put my suitcase down in this high, narrow room and look out on the crescent street where I am walking with the *Times,* one or two or three floors down, in the small hours when milk cartons are left at the doors of hotels, of this hotel, always the same, I look toward the trees of the park with its locked gates between the crescent street and the straight one,

look at the Lord John Russell a bit farther down Marchmont Street, on the right, its wooden sidewalk tables with one, two, or three not quite empty glasses of lukewarm beer abandoned a few minutes before closing time, its low chairs and very low rotten benches where we sit among the locals, almost inaudible and quasi inarticulate old gentlemen, and two or three girls dressed in unimaginable greens and pinks will chat with a waitress dressed in the same style,

look at the grey and brown Guinness foam spilled over the low table, the color of the wood the same as the best bitter, or perhaps so much spilled best bitter has given the wood the color of beer, close to that of the two or three pennies left on the table, in the crescent street where we walk at night on wet, brown leaves dropped from the trees of the locked park that are bare now and brown like the spilled beer on the low table of the Lord John Russell, we walk to the hotel door under the leafy and dark trees some night or other at the end of summer, some mild night in May, some night,

I pile the narrow bed in the high, narrow room with plastic bags full of books from Dillon's or Waterstone, from Books etc. murder one or Foyles, I take the books out one by one, lying on the bed, my head on the single narrow pillow placed vertically against the papered wall, the books stacked on the floor at the foot of the low bed, right by the door,

I close the door and put the newspaper down on the low bed, it is still night, or else the sun is crawling through the curtained window toward the bed, or else it is barely dawn, the wind rushing through trees armed with their first green or tearing off their end-of-August leaves, already less clinging, the rain beating the flagstones, and the wind sweeping into my room between the bottom of the (barely) sliding sash and the low sill above the radiator,

I open the door as soon as I hear the two peals of four notes, it is seven-thirty solar English winter time, and I go down to the cellar, the hotel basement, toward the smell of tea, bacon and toast, I look at the crescent street where I am walking, one or two or three floors below the window of the high and narrow room,

I look at the ceiling in the glimmering crescent of night in the room, in my vacant and vacuous night, for me alone the distant voice of Big Ben, once or twice or three, four times its four notes, descending only once,

I walk through Marchmont and Herbrand streets, through Montague Place, isolated amid the English voices low enough, anonymous enough, comprehensible only if I make an effort, I watch the city calmly give in to the dark, like a rural landscape with gentle distances, like the crescent street that I watch from my window as it plunges into the night,

with London plunging into the dark, with night falling, there is less noise, and sounds merge one by one from the mass, as if combed out by the night, I sit down on a bench in Russell Square, in a pool of light between trees, between the trees I see the sky, the source of light, the source of light is also the source of evening, the dark already black, already pitch black in the mass of trees, in the bushes of Russell Square, the nearest leaves perfectly outlined, defined against it, I see the light so feeble, so theatrical, so yellow as it fades, lingering in pockets on the crushed, still visible, fragrant grass,

London, limbo, "an absolutely inessential supplement to life," to my life, neither certainty nor comfort nor despair, words overheard lying on my back, once or twice or three, four times a year I lie down with an empty head under the yellow lamp, under the high ceiling of the narrow room, I listen to one or the other, or the full four quasi iambic four-note peals, the hour, the last hour of night, the wind rustling in the leaves of the trees lining the inner side of the crescent street, the sky ladling rain on the glass rectangle of the phone booth at the corner of Marchmont, over its green side (phone cards) (the last red booths are opposite Dillon's), the rainy night repeating "sorry, all lines are busy, sorry, all lines are busy,"

because here I am surrounded by the other language, because the voices are softer, because the threshold of understanding is a bit higher, the lamps in the nightly street weaker, more yellow, because I have nothing to do, to think here, only to hang on to the hours separated by the same four notes, once, twice, three, four times the same four notes deep in the quiet night in London where I come, in this hotel we come to, where I look at this photo taken from above, from an upper window, of me walking on the sidewalk of the crescent street, reading.

Coda

now I look out of the window
now I go out in the street
now I look out of the window

the street, a crescent of houses and trees
the sky, incompressible, takes a leap

now I look out of the window
now the street, empty and gone.

The Notebook

An empty notebook is like an abandoned head with nothing left in it: it used to be able to retain, but not any more. I intend to clutter this one with unprofitable traffic. And since you put it in my hands, I will fill it with a certain confusion of words, which ones, I don't yet know. And their fallout I'll, if possible, address: to you, telling their poverty, and to oblivion, exalting its calm scattering.

Don't be surprised if I decide to trammel it without so much as one illuminating through—a kind I don't possess. It is a maxim of the Sceptics that certainty cannot be based on reason. And yet I cannot keep this emptiness from having its effect on me. Some phrase will fall here; hence all are signaling. And just as the massive earth's invisible center violently draws me, so, at a given distance from all words, I have inexplicable affinities with some; there are invisible, yet solid paths on which one configuration touches off another and seems to lead right here. Do you not feel yourself the pull and expectation of some statement?

A loop has opened in these first pages, full of a silence impossible to ward off. It does not utter the kind of words that have remained secret from the beginnings. Nothing said here will be strange though common, unbelievable though certain, elevated though ordinary. Nothing profitable, nothing of value. It is an absolutely commonplace fate to receive a world as our share and not be enriched by it. In which mystery cult should I, year after year, have tracked its pattern entangled in disparate, supposedly harmonious contingencies? I have not come for offerings, but dispossession.

These words won't cause a stir, won't unseat the glory of colors, nor rival the effect of passing clouds at the end of day. A meditative construction, a plan to put forward their argument, is as deep as they go. Their method is slow sequence without ornament or exaltation: each page changes, continues into the next via similitude.

For in fact no world is ours. This is what the constant functioning of our mind tells us, against all propensity toward hope. Streets reveal it, encounters witness it, voices prove it. The unfolding of signs makes it evident. So abundant are these demonstrations that the refuge of white sheets, their promise of infinite, negative delights, seems a unique Gift granted by Him who Gives, if there is such a One. Come in through the window, floating through the panels of the mirror, along the pillows, the clouds. There.

There, you will no doubt read to mean: these lines in a notebook filled for you, the parabola of a dispatch bearing everywhere the question, "What's the matter?" To which, after long and ripe consideration you'd reply: "This," "this" for sure, because nothing visible can do better. Because if the world itself had been shown to us even just once, its aspect could not have failed to stupefy. But it will go otherwise and, no doubt, till the end.

A line still empty is of infinite dimensions: an infinite wall, I'd say, if the metaphor of an infinite wall were not too hackneyed to express this boundlessness. A narrow, interminable length, then, which is nothing, which could and, if it were, would be unprofitable. A loop, a torus, globules of incessant, boundless whiteness in a ring. In which every word, all words, will be lost.

Time is so obvious a determinant here that wise minds have taken this as proof of its linearity. But we enter and leave every line as if it had no before and progressively destroyed its after. As if every movement of the eye devoured it. Before us, white body of paper looking penetrable, behind us, black body of signs already overwhelmed by the infinite, vacant distance, where there revolve the planets of words under influence.

I would prefer not to interrupt at the edge of the page, not always to go back to these uneasy beginnings, these principles of unreality. And I would like to fill this notebook so solidly that the pages would be black from left to right and from top to bottom, but with legible fill. I would like to escape what is countable, escape enumeration. This would give me a kind of imbecile happiness, the kind felt by saints convinced of the terrible, amiable, blessed, grandiose, impenetrable and incomprehensible goodness of their God. It would perhaps be a delight homologous with staying between the sheets.

In every line there is intention to continue, continued intention, and deflection. Which, though they are essentially one and the same, are nevertheless assigned three separate manners. For every line of this piece of writing affects the following line and is at the same time inflected by it, just as it has affected the line preceding it. The current pulls it beyond itself even while it hastens to turn object. And destructive coherence wins out over a sober, fluid lightness.

So we should never summon up but what is extremely contemporary with the act of reading, the last word presented as if still followed by a blank, which your anticipation might fill with what light you please, though not with those phrases already congealed in a semblance of communication, the cursed future of the perfect. But everywhere, clearly, this trinity: the immobile, the already said, the forgotten.

Writing aspires to the levitation of the spoken word, which is far too lacking in seriousness and modesty. Here it is, heavy with meaning, running through secret passageways toward its object, but also as jammed as if not moving at all. Meaning before the line is the parent of meaning; after the line, meaning congeals. But the meaning we perceive, see, retain, proceeds from all three. We are both author and witness of this triple alliance.

Before tackling the first page, I took the small paper squares from cigarette packs that you had given me (I won't tell which) out of the grey envelope with the blue line seal and placed them on the page as obstacles: infinitely thin foils as if of a Riemann surface. This was the page in the empty notebook: "toute l'âme résumée / quand lente nous l'expirons / en plusieurs ronds de fumée / abolis en d'autres ronds / etc."*

Meaning is the tempter, meaning trickling from the line with the words addressing you: the address is the meaning. The meaning, incommensurable with the line, infinitely thin like the foil of a Riemann surface.

The meaning does not differ from the line (except in the infinitely negligible thickness of the paper pulled out of the rounds of smoke exhaled in expiation). The meaning does not diverge from the line, except perhaps in that completion precipitates and congeals it, whereas the line keeps going, and I will never reach its end. Neither will you.

---

*From Stéphane Mallarmé: "all of the soul summed up / as slowly we exhale it in / a few rings of smoke / that fade into other rings" —Trans. note.

Somber and vain and without comfort, the night. Somber and vain, the beginning of day. Unused, idle, the notebook long empty, like a dispossessed head. The leaden paste, the chalk ball of day against the windowpane. Nominal trees, stripped of their leaves by winter. We would need a large Seraphim, an infinite good, someOne. Would we?

Profitable silence is the measure of all things. Not the thumb-size sun, nor man, nor human beings. In silence, unformulated truths wait at the far end of lines never to be reached, understood, rhapsodized. Fearlessly, the silence of the written joins unwritten silence. To you this would no doubt mean snow, expectant snow, taciturn, borne in through the window, caught in the panels of the mirror, toward the bed blown.

Where the read notebook will again be empty, as if it had always been.

Other Books by Jacques Roubaud available from Dalkey Archive

The Great Fire of London: A Story with Interpolations and Bifurcations. Translated by Dominic Di Bernardi.
A hypertextlike novel concerning the author's attempt to cope with his wife's death and his struggles to write a book about it. "Incomparable . . . as fascinating as life itself" (Harry Mathews). "Roubaud has finally produced the book that his great and varied talent had always promised" (Gabriel Josipovici, *The Independent*). 330 pages. **Cloth, $21.95; paper, $12.95.**

Hortense in Exile. Translated by Dominic Di Bernardi.
In this sequel to *Hortense Is Abducted* (below), our beautiful heroine finds herself enmeshed in a parody of *Hamlet*. "An *opéra bouffe* of novelistic conventions . . . a droll burlesque of literary forms" (*Booklist*). "It's *The Mouse That Roared* by way of Derrida" (*Kirkus*). 211 pages. **Cloth, $19.95.**

Hortense Is Abducted. Translated by Dominic Di Bernardi.
A comic detective novel in the tradition of Queneau and Calvino. "Impishly fantastic" (*Atlantic*). "The translation is excellent and captures the truly Rabelaisian *joie de vivre* of the narrative" (*Library Journal*). "Interlaced with learned allusions, mathematical clues and formulas . . . most welcome" (*Booklist*). 229 pages. **Cloth, $19.95.**

The Princess Hoppy, or, The Tale of Labrador. Translated by Bernard Hœpffner.
A postmodern fairy tale and a giddy inquiry into reading literary texts. A "farrago of Monty Python, Barthelme's *Snow White, Through the Looking-Glass* and 'The Hunting of the Snark'" (*Kirkus*). "[In] this delightfully eccentric book, Mr. Roubaud combines a nimble intellect with an endearingly buoyant spirit" (*New York Times Book Review*). 132 pages. **Paper, $9.95.**

Some Thing Black. Translated by Rosmarie Waldrop.
Prose poems about the death of a loved one and the process of grief. "No work of recent French poetry, indeed of recent French literature, is more moving . . . a lasting work of art" (*Asylum*). "Waldrop's fine translation is a tribute to Roubaud's rich and often lyrical meditations on death" (*Library Journal*). 144 pages + 17 pages of photographs. **Cloth, $19.95.**

Available at better bookstores or directly from the publisher: add $3.00 postage and handling to all orders and send check or money order to Dalkey Archive Press, Campus Box 4241, Normal, IL 61790-4241. Credit card orders call (309) 438-7555.